ELSE

by Solomon Goudsward

ISBN: 978-1-989940-24-2
Copyright © 2021 Solomon Goudsward
Dimensionfold Publishing
Prince George BC CAN
dimensionfold.com

For someone else.

ELSE

what I'm getting to

home is home as log hom
            logos homos
           a homolog
     (s as two as three
     as if you want to)

lo goes a log house
a locus poke us

a focus
on the family   at home

a logos polka
see where I get to
walk with walk with me
where I go

        home is
        homing
     go home with me
     come   with me
        home

home as come
    as to come
        coming home

home comes
         home
home homes
homecoming/homehoming
to home as to   yes

where
      it   comes together
    all

everything you've done
        you're done
done home
dome home

do   me   who me?

home is in time
home comes in time
home at the end
the end as what comes

the ing of end
    in the inging

can you see the ing
or/of the ed?

home is eding ing

what else?

this is about me
home is about me
ho(me)
        here and there

what comes
what else
what elses

        we come where we go
        we come a way
        to go a way

a way to home
        to come

to go as a way
to home
to be homing

the beginning of home is
the end of home
is a door
a way in or else

home has rooms
home as rooms
home has
home has as home as

home alone
a lone home to phone

phone a room
log room
what keeps it all
                home

log as log
   os log
       os

    has room ?
              s
home ends at h
        at e

what you want
comes home from work
with dinner

hands folded papers
in post-Biblican liturgies

the place you are
and what is to be
discovered and had

have and to have
              had
in the end

you like to want to
you want to like too

what you want
is built to be
but be is out
overstocking the end now
the contents of a happy life
time slips, lippery with words

clean up the home
and everything
looks in order
to find
what is   out

skeletons in the yard
yard out in the world

drive   way
    gives
to parking

organ house
organ doors
organ eyes
on the road   a head
a row of heads
outside in the road

where you're trying to get
              to(get(her
                    to be/come

here in t(here

you would love her
if she drove a way

a thin noth(ing
vapour hanged over
charges of
     (ing

inimal animask
prutting around
long grass in the eaves
a suisiding vinyl
let down to a leveling
ground   truth in your teeth
grinding to wake the dead

no story
told in formal
kitchenscratch
but of snakes
a movement side to side
but forward
scaling x axis

an image, you think
of brownbottle
foil, thread of mouth
that was that and
dark waters vibe rating
nothing to tell about
nothing happens later

later you pick it up
asking where it went
silence a swarm of
unseen mosquitos
glinting the air
in your basement suite

just play
a hanging in the balance
the two-inch wall
of the sandbox
grainy dirtberg
sub-merged
in a parcel of land
what was received
in the beginning
but as loose change
into Styrofoam cups

victory is to sleep
behind one's self and dream
with suspicion of
eves dropping

their odd evening
two: one and one too
through your underwater caverns
and ancient libraries
on the other side
of the atoms

to see a mirror
and wonder more
unable to make out a visage
and so to close one's
eyes and plant the forehead
against the glass
half-what
emptiful for the spirit

it is difficult to escape
possibility as a dwelling place
       (as a place that dwells
deeply in all directions
expectral hauntings
like 2x4s
like a shifting rib
in a mobile home
the spiraling centre
dispossessed of itself

feel two legs or more
as a way to stand up
omnied/erectional
spermanent structures in overlap
lap
    up the posabilities
around an ass fault
                     track
ing futures
ahead of the curve sssss

home as who?
dwelling in the bodies of time
plastic tic tic
          talk just talk
          no seconds
no minute de-tailings
just track
tracks pressable to circle
silvery with empty

centre unmoving
listen just listen
engines cycling a round home

else is something
to be doing

home a loan
taken out
to the backyard and buried
you can't take anything
there is nothing for you
to do here

else is more
often   then not

an obituary
self-addressed

what to do later
is here for you now
as a sickness
glassy beads form in your palms
a handy pair of clams
reaching for the doorknob

you will not survive
complete satisfaction

buoyant voice
a falling angel, drumbeat
to the punch
repeat bell, chime in
you and you all over
you're in the rice
eaten/eating
by yourself
all aloan

the technique for to be:
    recognize the things you can do
    pick up an object and move it
    speak to anyone

there is so much.
let it all be
   hanging like an indent
ation in your eye
I'm saying
burn down philosophy
start playing cards

un deux trois pour la bruit
de le jeu
you sling your influence
across a popsicle stick
bridge to the chorus
to the verse about gods enduring
faithfulness

t(here's so much.
what else?

long langue
trailing behind
languette over what's over
you spoke the words into the dust
the future lies
devirginized before
the backs of your heels
scabs heeling loyally
alongside as you
                    go

you knew few commands
sit stay stray
but there is no return
no theo reticle
re(course to complete
or replete with content
                      meant to
                      heal

the past is a(head
without a mouth
you can't speak to it

what was as what could be
or will have been
a testament to restless hope
a test, a call
        a ball to roll
a round in your hands

get over   what's over?
the past presents future

of course of course
as a series of obstacles
or a selection of homes:
over come or come over
but never without
appropriate acommandations

speak your tracks
into having been
spread out before you
all this time

uno does très bien
mais we walk on hand
            in hand
oh you love what's coming
to you   has been given
the weight of empty chests
pounding dutiful
your eyes telescopes

the subject has been brooched
with pearls
the future decided
              ly nebulous
a lens seen
        through
              to the end
              to the ed of you

p(resent
what has been given
you (everything)

there is nothing else

a soft finger on your shoulder
and you turn round
to roll through the days
a threshing hold
now against someday soon
deferred: pulled away fer
godssake
do you have to look
do you half two

tomorrow row
gently down
merrily we roll a log
uphill (both ways, both sides of today)
"one must imagine
Sisyphus in rain boots
splashing   storm fractals
the universe in particle or
something along your line
hook and sink her
fingers still tracing
spectral epaulettes
you'd ram your tongue down
tomorrow   if only
she would come

come along on a holiday
(less holy now
                it necessitates movement)
come and leave
home a pilgrim

wondering the hillside
down to a point
of arrival

come log a holiday
clearcut with image machinery
taking steps to preserve what
may now not be lost

log as take
or keep
hidden a way
to remember

leave and come
home a grim pill
                to swallow
home comes to terms:
"ceci n'est pas une maison"
a home is called

call home
        on holiday
a home to call to
a hall to come to

log as take as talk
a way for later

weigh the days
on a large scale
reproduction of a log house
photo albums of deadfall
in the living room
the points taken
for a structure

now for later
and everything else

home a shrine
in the distance
               between
yes   and   no

n   o   w

the soft opening of a word
a breath in the space of lips
YeahWeigh

HHHHHHhhhh

open to the phonics of silence
of God, the shared breath
of a severed family
a heavy silence
in the dinning room

the distaste between y and s
a simile of feathered heads
an e flies peak to peak
executed in the mouth
but spilling out
          spelling out a predicative
                      pre-dictable
in the time before it takes

say ing and it arrives
iting on the tong
                ue

    the mute diction
        mutediction
            mutiction
                mutition
                    mutation

say ed and it is
iteding through particools
            partycoolers
              grab a beer and chuggugug

iteding edited to an orthodoxy
straight laced and you read and hear
selections from a cat, a log
a bird, a room, a house, a home
I would not could not
if I tried
to lebark a dog
(or wait, have I?

living (in) the distents
be tween
new and newer
now and nower and nowest

no west but not east
no rth but not
somewhere else in space

HHHHGhhhhh remember?
the worst thing is to get
what you're lookin for

talking on the phone newskool
with the smirking avatarted
girl and you in the red hat

no hat   that I know
no real connection

look but don't
             find
keep it else   where?

                w her e

                    w   e
                      her

                      we
                     h e r e

                                    e

                                             eeeee

a catalogue of present impressions
has slipped behind
the refrigerator

full of blood
in vile arrangements
vibrations of an electric heart

everything lies
behind the fridge
it all disappears immediately

letters of letters
let loose
across post-post
              all service
talk to you delater

letter see you naked
in paperclipped photo
printed, paperlipped
      ripped later
         down the mid dle

you were trying too talk
through folded
tongues preserved in a card
              board box
licked the stamp like
an ice cream cone

no, it wasn't your flesh
hanging off itself
for life   death or
what comes

letter read you
      redo   into a certain future

let letter lettest
(there are three ways to be
with increasing difficulty

al(low   a lowering to form

multicoloured fridge magnets
spilling out a mess(age
a heap of lines
           in lines

the maximum allowable letestation
a letting of blood into envelopes

eventually everything gets sent

a tent
in the desert
the arc hive of the permanent
hides from the sun
logos goes camping

logoes the locust
through the dusty air
out of manna
            festival destiny
pharaoh builds a grave for later now

comes sailing in
the arkhive the firmament
firm cave of treasures
a lens of the earthly eye

or a honeybee hex
bugs swarming   a
town ship
the land is   gone

bugs forming/farming the land
block by block to the ground

firmament: home dome

a sky scalp over mind
       (the space of predictation
       over matter

bees in the archive
sweet pages stick together

curse, curses, cursament

or, sweeter
a hive in a hollow log

it is a condition of the moment
to be seen   through
seeing through
the last thing the bird never saw

prey to a proaching momentum
now is a dead bird
decomposing
on the porch

we should repent
why aren't we all writing
each other   poetry all the time
walking around with music
projected onto grainy surfaces

see that a street is not magnetic
and a sidewalk is the same as a roadsign
poured over the ground
there is nothing in lines
which says follow or stay
there are no lines

a pothole is a percussive digression
on an imaginary line
where do you think
you're going
down
                      in the degradation
              of asphalt there is a kind (of)
        liberation of unimagined planes
their surfaces projected onto our surfaces
musically

we should rep   ent
                res

home a knot
tied in a line
roads take you else(where?

else took you out for dinner
ordered your favourites
alphabetically and whispered
in your ear   promises
that the living moment would never arrive

she is sly in her disappearances
you turn around and you are
wearing her clothes

you have declared
the limits endlessly
you have crossed
out diagrams
for past futures
you are sitting still
in the middle of the carpet
breathing candle wax
avoiding the questions which follow
you like a bad memory

is there anything which escapes
being folded into a progression?

you are becoming more tranquil
which may serve you
in future careers
is there anything that is not
                                      a step
                    a step
        a step
stop
you release every inclination
but the inclination to release
trapped in a manual
you cannot control
what you are

thoughts like cars and cars
like thoughts like books
on a falling shelf

everything goes

you have declared
the limits endless
the infinite stopping

every long thrum of the house
inharmony   without
(how appurtenances are added
in negation of negation)
              with(out)
the formation of a chord
or the tying of a knot
for grip

eyes closed to see
your dark eyelids
a gauche presentation
of the lie
of concealment

you practice a habitation
of the place
behind the bridge
of your nose
play as a group
of kids smoking
out of view
of the highway
on the carpeted floor

visions projected on the lids
to embellish a closing
eye as jar
as receptacle
take in to keep in
near the limit of
what isn't you
or what is

locate yourself at the edge of the skin
as a totality
for the sake of nothing
forsake nothing
nothinging at each step
not hinging, a whole of non-steps unswung
you could interiorize a non-articulation
of not non-articles
or almost anything else
unimaginable

dedeclare, let clarity
not be not unspoken but
ringing heavy throughout
the living room air
like microscopic insects
concealed in the carpet

someone else will be/come
home to you
the opening of their soft doors
mute in the inner room of your breath

ELSING

now you are driving to work
now you are driving work
now you are work
now you work
now work
now
no
o
on
won
you won
won work
work won you
work won driving you
work won driving you to

kill or be kissed
or look for a new car
                     eer

looking out the window   now
the grass is leaming with it all
and your cellular laminations
send you forward
               ed as an email
boxes re: sponding to each other

you want to be anywhere   else

fulfilling the unrequited
              requirement
to work
towards
to words
       too often spoking
work takes time
in circles
work keeps time
your foot tapping
imp patiently weighting
a burden   the hand

hands as steps, steppers
hands as feet
walking across a cobblestone
path of letters stacked
like bricks to build work
there is space outside
and escape beneath
your middle finger

bring work home
work from home
due monday
do twosday
one day
soon or else

is there any space that is not an escapescape?

a/void a domisill
a silly skillset
work at dom
labe or relations
label orations
labial rations
lappellations
window sillow talk

l'appel au travail
        travel to work
on a line
strapped to
a tree with routes
work as position
        pose-ition in escapespace

postitution in stinktuitive markings
a rub to make it afishoil
you have become something   else

then you get to

leave or go or come

but don't ask where it all comes   to

in a vowel there is a gloating chasm
chiastic in resounding   o   o
through atoms

there is a limit to the finitude
of divisibility: the endless being of whatever
there is

you have said all this before
(but how can anything stop?)

o o o

when you can feel the endless space of your bones
and there is a heavy crunch of destitudinal walls
like a trash comp actor
                playing indivisibility
                        in visibilitidy grid griddle
a broad flat surface heated by natural energies
with both residential and
commercial applications

a ply to be an actor
(or not to be)
propagating vowel movements
see yourself as a planeopomorphized human
animal screaming
squish squash o o

the unborn off spring
offspred out on a brood
fat surface
cooking
coo king never to fly
an unborn bird
roasted by a plane

you could be/come
obsessed with the white and yellow o of an egg
frying/flying on a plane
stare into the endless yellow
and reconsider
"for my birdin is easy
and my yolk is light

       white as a fetter
       yolk us folks
       with eyes to see
       and ears to here
            to there
       a man, amen

eggsistents
becoming home
a shell to break
out of   a sexual act
of emergence
>   see
the egg tent of meeting
the world in its mediating finality
all homes are eggs frying in the sun

you grow up
and work in cubation
to mature
like a fine crotch whisk
>   see
fitting sitting in a barrel
completing competing tasks
get a raise and
jerk from home
no egg to master
just ink to cubate

you can draw
a picture of yourself
in future tents
and wonder
where you've been

work to go
a way on vocation
a grate   a scape

the stale gutterances of walls
in the home/office

vacate as a project
of a voidance
practice a void dance
work at playing
play at work
per formance
for permanence
become a statue
of yourself
           working

work to text
pre-position yourself in/to a future tense
labial labour amortalized
over a fixed period.
(who broke it in the ~~first~~ place?
what place in time?)

work for text
a statue of limitations
a sheet spread over a ghost
lying mortified
this is the photo album of work
the appearance of death
as a present

death is pre-sent
through the post
as a reap resentation
what else to do
before becoming amortal
    amour to all
    or fall armoured
    a dull morass
      more ass than face

the body's end:
  an asshole in the ground
    as a home
    worked for

    year after year

                    work the g(round
                    untill the soil
                    works for you
dig a foundation
    as if it were there allready
    an absent absence
    in the ground
                ation
        round
                        to mortal eyes
                        a "place" as a place

pour a debasement
sweet concrete lumps
the limits of a hardening room
                a tomb
                a womb
                        to return to

        no escape

live to see
the body's ending

you are a thing inging
toward nothing else

else moves
you all around
in loosening spirals
all you ever want
to do is something else

where you're going
        going from a to
                to a
                two
                to too
        going from a four
                  six
                      eight
        growing from a form
        a golden fork in a road

        a tender decade later
        you remember where it was
        you came out of
        today was tomorrow yesterday
        a dozen lines in the sand
        to remember the limit less
        retreat of the sun

else moves you
along/across lines
and back to the point
of a longing/a crossing
to look beyond as a transgression

a return to I
once more a peering
to I as else
what are we getting
                        to?
home there
to sleep   off a cliff
              if you want
                            to
go to come to go to
              sleep
              or else

www.ingramcontent.com/pod-product-compliance
Lightning Source LLC
Chambersburg PA
CBHW072039080526
44578CB00007B/537